"SEE YOU NEXT WEDNESDAY," SAID A. D. HARE, MD.

"THURSDAY," THE NARCISMOUSE CORRECTED FLATLY.

"I'M ALWAYS SO SAD WHEN IT'S OVER," MOANED THE BIPOLARBEAR.

"BUT WE LITERALLY JUST STARTED," THE NARCISMOUSE REPLIED SHARPLY.

"OH, RIGHT. WE DID," SAID A. D. HARE, MD, BLINKING IN SURPRISE.

"GREAT, I'M SO EXCITED," SAID THE BIPOLARBEAR. "I THINK."

FOURTH.

WELCOME, EVERYONE, TO OUR FIFTH SESSION!

"OUR FOURTH SUPPORT GROUP SESSION,"
REPEATED A. D. HARE, MD.

"OH GAWHD, MY HEAWT!" GASPED THE HYPOHIPPO, STARTLED, AS A FEW PILLS PLOPPED OUT OF ITS MOUTH.

"THAT WAS THE DOOR," GRUMBLED THE BORDERCOLLIE.

"COME IN."

KNOCK

"COME IIIIN!"

KNOCK

COOOOME IIIIINNNN!!!

"'Scuse me. I'm late, ate," blurted the Gnurette as it stumbled through the door.

"Not a problem, we were just about to leave," said A. D. Hare, MD.

"Start," corrected the NarcisMouse.

"That's what I meant."

"Where should I sit, it, HOO?" asked the Gnurette.

"Lie down over there," suggested A. D. Hare, MD.

"Sit. Sit on the chair next to me," the NarcisMouse proposed.

"Or that," mumbled A. D. Hare, MD.

"THERE'S NOTHING WRONG WITH HIM,"
HUFFED THE BorderCollie.

"NOW THAT WE'RE ALL HERE,
LET'S PICK UP WHERE WE LEFT OFF LAST WEDNESDAY,"
INTERRUPTED A. D. HARE, MD.
"THURSDAY," THE NarcisMouse CORRECTED SHARPLY.

"LAST THURSDAY," A. D. HARE, MD REPEATED, SOUNDING UNCERTAIN.
"THE THURSDAY BEFORE LAST," THE NarcisMouse ADDED, UNFLINCHING.

"WHERE WE LEFT OFF THE THURSDAY BEFORE LAST,"
A. D. HARE, MD CONCLUDED.

"'I TOLD YOU ABOUT HOW I TWIRL PIROUETTES IN THE MOONLIGHT," THE BIPOLARBEAR REPORTED, BEAMING WITH PRIDE.

"GOOD, THEN LET'S PICK UP FROM THERE," SAID A. D. HARE, MD.
"EVERYONE, SHARE SOMETHING YOU'RE ESPECIALLY GOOD AT."

"THEN IT'S MY TURN," DECLARED THE NARCISMOUSE PROMPTLY.

"TURN FOR WHAT?" ASKED A. D. HARE, MD.
"FOR SHARING," SIGHED THE NARCISMOUSE.
"OH, RIGHT," MUMBLED A. D. HARE, MD

"I'M PARTICULARLY SKILLED AT STANDING IN FRONT OF THE MIRROR AND ADMIRING MYSELF FROM EVERY ANGLE. WITHOUT BLINKING," THE NARCISMOUSE ANNOUNCED PROUDLY.

"CU, CU, CUCUMBER KING! HOO?" THE GNURETTE BLURTED OUT.
"THANKS, BOTH OF YOU! AND WHAT ABOUT YOU?"
A. D. HARE, MD TURNED TOWARD THE HYPOHIPPO EXPECTANTLY.

"I CAN TAFTE THE COLOR OF MY PILLF," SAID THE HYPOHIPPO THROUGH A MOUTHFUL, TOSSING IN TWO MORE TABLETS FOR GOOD MEASURE.

"BLUE AND RED."

"WONDERFUL!" EXCLAIMED THE BIPOLARBEAR ENTHUSIASTICALLY.
"YOU'RE DOING AN ABSOLUTELY AMAZING JOB!"

"SOUNDS LIKE QUITE THE RARE TALENT," MUSED A. D. HARE, MD THOUGHTFULLY.
"AND WHAT ABOUT YOU?"

HE TURNED TO THE BORDERCOLLIE.

"GOOD," SAID A. D. HARE, MD, NODDING WITH SATISFACTION.

"NOW THAT WE'VE ALL INTRODUCED OURSELVES, WE CAN MOVE ON TO THE NEXT EXERCISE."

"IFF IT FAFE?" ASKED THE HYPOHIPPO NERVOUSLY, A PILL SLIPPING OUT OF ITS MOUTH.

"AS LONG AS YOU STAY CALM AND DON'T SWAT AT IT, YOU'LL BE FINE... OR SO I'VE HEARD," SAID A. D. HARE, MD VAGUELY.

"THE EXERCISE! IS THAT DANGEROUS?"
THE NARCISMOUSE INTERJECTED FIRMLY.

"OH," SAID A. D. HARE, MD SLOWLY, DRAGGING HIS GAZE AWAY FROM THE BEE HOVERING AT THE WINDOW.

"NO, THE EXERCISE ISN'T DANGEROUS. AT LEAST... AS FAR AS I CAN REMEMBER."

A. D. Hare, MD, started rummaging
through his bag.
And rummaged.
And rummaged.
And then sat completely still.

Everyone stared intently at A. D. Hare, MD, who sat motionless.

A. D. Hare, MD shook his head briefly and pulled out a crumpled piece of paper.

"Hunts make me unbearably sad,"
grumbled the BipolarBear, his voice cracking.

"Trea, Trea,"
the BorderCollie clamped a paw over the GnuRette's mouth.
"Moo? Glig, glag, bnaRB!"

"This paper holds the clue to where we'll find the treasure,"
said A. D. Hare, MD, waving the crumpled note triumphantly.

"I'll read it," declared the NarcisMouse, snatching it out of his hand.

"NOW WE NEED TO FIGURE OUT TOGETHER WHERE THE TREASURE MIGHT BE,"
EXPLAINED A. D. HARE, MD.

"THAT'S SO BEAUTIFUL,"
CHIMED IN THE BIPOLARBEAR, HIS EYES GLISTENING.

"BUT IT'S LITERALLY WRITTEN RIGHT THERE! ON THE DAMN
BENCH IN FRONT OF THE DAMN HOUSE!"
BARKED THE BORDERCOLLIE, COMPLETELY LOSING IT.

"HE'S FINE!" BARKED THE BorderCollie.

"LET'S JUST GO FIND THE TREASURE,"
THE NarcisMouse CUT IN DRYLY.
"I'LL LEAD."

THE WHOLE GROUP ROSE TO THEIR FEET.
THE Gnurette SAT BACK DOWN.
THEN STOOD UP.
SAT AGAIN.
FINALLY STOOD AND SHUFFLED AFTER THE OTHERS.

"HOLD ON," SAID THE HypoHippo, METICULOUSLY APPLYING SUNSCREEN TO ITS FOREHEAD.
"OKAY. NOW."

EVERYONE HEADED OUT THE DOOR.
TOWARD THE PARK BENCH.

ARRIVED.

"BUT IT HAS TO BE HERE," SAID A. D. HARE, MD.
"THE MAN ON THE RADIO SAID SO."

"NOTHING IN SIGHT," SNIFFLED THE BIPOLARBEAR.
"EXCEPT THAT GORGEOUS BIRD OVER THERE ON THE TREE! SO COLORFUL! SO VIB-
RANT!" THE BIPOLARBEAR BEAMED.

EVERYONE TURNED TO LOOK AT THE PARAPARROT.

"WHAT?" THE PARAPARROT ASKED,
EYEING THE GNURETTE SUSPICIOUSLY.

"HAVE YOU SEEN A TREASURE?"
THE NARCISMOUSE INTERJECTED, ANNOYED.

"NONSENSE," THE NarcisMOUSE SAID COOLLY.

"WE'RE ON A TREASURE HUNT. THE CLUE SAYS THE TREASURE SHOULD BE HERE SOMEWHERE. HAVE YOU SEEN IT?"

"YEAH, TOTALLY," CHIMED IN THE GNURETTE.

"THE TREASURE'S GOTTA BE HERE. CLICK, CLACK."

"A TREASURE, HUH?" THE ParaParrot WHISPERED CONSPIRATORIALLY, FLUTTERING GRACEFULLY DOWN FROM THE TREE.

"I MIGHT'VE SEEN SOMETHING LIKE THAT. COME CLOSER, AND I'LL TELL YOU WHERE IT IS."

Everyone gathered around the ParaParrot.

The HypoHippo hung back a little. Just to be safe.

A GREEN PILL TUMBLED OUT OF
THE HYPOHIPPO'S MOUTH IN SHOCK.

"I SAW SOMEONE WALKING OFF WITH IT.
VERY SLOWLY,"
THE PARAPARROT ANNOUNCED PROUDLY.

"WHERE DID HE GO?"
THE NARCISMOUSE ASKED IMPATIENTLY.

"I COULD TELL YOU,"
THE PARAPARROT REPLIED,
PAUSING DRAMATICALLY.

AWKWARD SILENCE.

OFF TO THE HILL OVER THERE.

The BorderCollie marched ahead with determination.

The others followed in silence.

FINALLY, THEY REACHED THE HILL.

"WE'RE ON A TREASURE HUNT!"

THE BipolarBear EXCLAIMED, PRACTICALLY BOUNCING WITH EXCITEMENT.

"ABSOLUTELY NOT!"

CRIED THE Post-Traumadillo IN HORROR.

"I'M STAYING RIGHT HERE AND SHUTTING MY, MY EYES TIGHT."

"TH-THIS IS THE ONLY PLACE WHERE I'M SAFE,"
THE POST-TRAUMADILLO STAMMERED, VOICE TREMBLING.
"EVERYWHERE ELSE, I'VE HAD... AWFUL, AWFUL EXPERIENCES."

"OH MY. WHAT HAPPENED?" THE HYPOHIPPO ASKED NERVOUSLY.

"A MISADDRESSED LETTER HERE, A PACKAGE TOO HEAVY THERE, AND A BARKING DOG OVER
YONDER. UGH... I'D RATHER NOT TALK ABOUT IT. IT WAS JUST SO... HORRIFYING!"
THE POST-TRAUMADILLO WAILED.
"IF I EVER HAVE TO LEAVE THIS HILL AGAIN, MY REKINDLED MEMORIES WILL SURELY BE THE
DEATH OF ME!"

"THAT SOUNDS AMAZING!" THE BIPOLARBEAR CHIMED IN, BEAMING.

"W-WHAT?" THE POST-TRAUMADILLO'S EYES WIDENED IN SHOCK, TEARS BRIMMING.

"Maybe you can still help us find the treasure,"
the NarcisMouse suggested, trying to distract the Post-Traumadillo.
"It's been stolen, and the thief must have passed by here."

"A... a thief?" The Post-Traumadillo shivered, sniffing loudly.
"Earlier, some strange figure tried to climb the hill...
fell a few times... and then just shuffled off like nothing happened."

"HOO? HIDE, HIDE, HIDEAWAY! SNARF!"
CRIED THE GNURETTE EXCITEDLY, TAPPING ITS HEAD THREE TIMES.

"EXACTLY," SAID THE NARCISMOUSE WITH A SHARP NOD.
"THAT MUST HAVE BEEN THE MALEFACTOR!"

"WHO'F GOT MALAIFE?" WHISPERED THE HYPOHIPPO NERVOUSLY.

THE BORDERCOLLIE ROLLED HIS EYES.

"WE'RE ALL FINE," THE NarcisMouse REASSURED THE GROUP.

"THE THIEF WON'T BE ONCE I GET MY PAWS ON HIM!" SNARLED THE BorderCollie.

"BUT WHICH TRAIN ARE WE CATCHING NOW?" ASKED A. D. Hare, MD, SUDDENLY.

"WHAT TRAIN?" ASKED THE Post-Traumadillo, LOOKING UTTERLY BAFFLED.

"HE MEANS WHERE THE THIEF RAN OFF TO," CLARIFIED THE NarcisMouse.

"THAT TOO," MUMBLED A. D. Hare, MD, VAGUELY.

"OH! RIGHT. HERE, ON MY DANGER MAP... I MARKED THE SPOT WITH AN X,"
SAID THE POST-TRAUMADILLO PROUDLY, HOLDING UP THE MAP.

"Everyfing's marked on here,"
observed the HypoHippo, crunching on a tablet.

The Post-Traumadillo stared at its map,
as if squinting might make it less useless.

"That... is indeed correct,"
it muttered, defeated.

"THANK YOU FROM THE BOTTOM OF MY HEART!"
THE BIPOLARBEAR EXCLAIMED,
SPREADING HIS ARMS WIDE TO HUG THE POST-TRAUMADILLO.

"ST-STAY BACK! DON'T COME NEAR ME!"
THE POST-TRAUMADILLO SHRIEKED,
CURLING ITSELF EVEN TIGHTER INTO A BALL.

THE BIPOLARBEAR SETTLED FOR PATTING WHAT HE ASSUMED WAS ITS SHOULDER INSTEAD.

THE POST-TRAUMADILLO BEGAN
TO SLOWLY ROLL AWAY.

EVERYONE SPUN AROUND AND BOLTED TOWARD THE FOREST AS FAST AS THEY COULD.

Soon, a clearing emerged ahead.

"Dat one right dere... fat muft be him!"
whispered the HypoHippo nervously, crunching another pill.

"Looks tired," observed A. D. Hare, MD.

"Probably from running,"
added the NarcisMouse
matter-of-factly.

"LET. ME." THE DEPRESSDONKEY MUTTERED FLATLY, NOT EVEN LIFTING HIS HEAD.

"HAND OVER THAT TREASURE, EAZURE! HOO? DOWELDWARF! SNARF!"
THE GNURETTE SCREECHED, FLAILING DRAMATICALLY.

"EVERYTHING. POINTLESS."
THE DEPRESSDONKEY REPLIED IN A
MONOTONE, HIS EYES HALF-CLOSED.

"MARVELOUS!"
THE BIPOLARBEAR
BEAMED WITH
DELIGHT.

"I don't think that's how it works,"
the NarcisMouse observed,
its voice dripping with saccharine sweetness.
"Could you please give us back our treasure?"

"Everything. Hurts,"
the DepressDonkey murmured weakly.

"Iff got fomething for pain,"
the HypoHippo offered eagerly,
swiftly popping a red pill
into the DepressDonkey's mouth.

"It'th working," declared the HypoHippo enthusiastically.
"I'll give him anofer!"

Without missing a beat,
it added a yellow pill
with the precision of a seasoned pharmacist.

"SOMEONE HAS IT. TOOK IT AWAY,"
THE DepressDonkey REPLIED, LIFELESSLY.

"NOT AGAIN," GROANED A. D. HARE, MD.
"HOW ARE WE SUPPOSED TO KEEP TRACK
OF ANYTHING AT THIS RATE?"

"GIVE HIM ANOTHER," ORDERED THE BorderCollie, ENTIRELY UNFAZED.

WITH PRACTICED EFFICIENCY, THE HypoHippo TOSSED A BLUE PILL INTO THE DepressDonkey'S MOUTH.

"CARRYING A LARGE CHEST. OUT OF THE FOREST," THE DepressDonkey ADDED, FLAT AS EVER.

"WHAT DID HE LOOK LIKE? WHEN WAS THIS? AND WHERE DID HE GO?"
THE BorderCollie BARKED AT THE DepressDonkey, BEFORE TURNING TO THE HypoHippo.
"STOP HOLDING BACK, KEEP 'EM COMING!"

THE HypoHippo SIGHED SOFTLY, RUMMAGED THROUGH ITS STASH, AND PULLED OUT THREE BLUE,
ONE GREEN, TWO WHITE, ONE RED, AND TWO YELLOW PILLS. WITHOUT HESITATION, IT POPPED THEM
INTO THE DepressDonkey'S MOUTH.

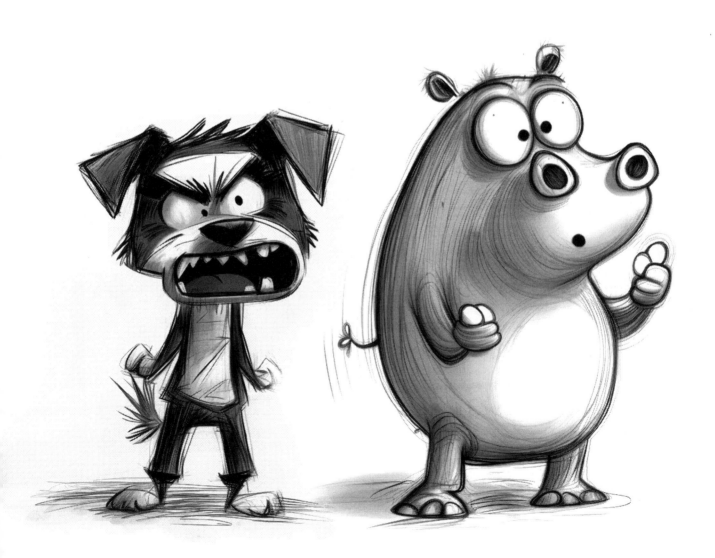

"YOU BROKE HIM,"

A. D. HARE, MD STATED PLAINLY, GIVING THE DEPRESSDONKEY A CAUTIOUS POKE WITH A STICK.

NO REACTION.

"HE'LL BE FINE,"
THE BORDERCOLLIE SAID WITH A SHRUG, GLANCING AT THE HYPOHIPPO,
WHO MERELY SHRUGGED BACK, SILENTLY SORTING ITS PILLS.

"LET'S KEEP MOVING BEFORE THE THIEF GETS TOO FAR AHEAD,"
THE NARCISMOUSE SUGGESTED.
"HE CAN'T HAVE GOTTEN FAR."

The group hurried toward the gray house in the east.
Eventually, they all arrived, slightly out of breath.

"This house looks familiar,"
said A. D. Hare, MD, scratching his head thoughtfully.

"This is where we started,"
the NarcisMouse sighed, exasperated.

"THE DOOR, OOR'S WIDE OPEN. CLICK, CLACK!"
SHOUTED THE GNURETTE, SLAMMING THE DOOR SHUT, THEN OPENING IT AGAIN,
SHUTTING IT ONCE MORE, AND REOPENING IT YET AGAIN.

"LIFTEN," WHISPERED THE HYPOHIPPO. "THERE'TH THOMEONE INTHIDE."

"LET'S GET 'EM!"
BARKED THE BORDERCOLLIE, STORMING THROUGH THE DOOR.

THE REST OF THE GROUP RUSHED IN AFTER HIM.

INSIDE STOOD SOMEONE HOLDING A TREASURE CHEST TIGHTLY.

"HAND BACK OUR TREASURE!"

SNAPPED THE BORDERCOLLIE, RAISING HIS PAWS MENACINGLY.

"WHAT?" ASKED THE WHALEZHEIMER'S, BLINKING AT THEM IN UTTER CONFUSION.

"Our treasure!"

The NarcisMouse clarified once more.

"How?"

asked the Whalezheimer's, examining the chest as if it had just appeared in its arms.

"Don't act dumb, umb! HOO?"

the Gnurette shouted, flailing its arms wildly.

"Toss over that chest. SNARF!"

"Who?"

asked the Whalezheimer's, glancing around cluelessly.

"Thomething'th not right with him," mumbled the HypoHippo worriedly.

THE BipolarBear
chuckled happily to himself,
swaying side to side.

THE HypoHippo
reluctantly put its pills away.

"Why did you steal our chest?" growled the BorderCollie, glaring at the Whalezheimer's.

"'Stealing' is a bit... subjective," mumbled A. D. Hare, MD, taking a cautious step back.

"Subjective?" The NarcisMouse spun around, fixing him with a sharp glare.
"Are you kidding me right now?"

"Well, you know... 'stealing' is a broad term..." A. D. Hare, MD began nervously.

"WHAT WOULD YOU CALL IT THEN?" the BorderCollie demanded loudly.

"Taking care of it... and maybe walking around with it a little?"
offered A. D. Hare, MD sheepishly.

""Looking after it... and walking around a bit?" The NarcisMouse repeated incredulously. "Are you telling me you knew all along he had the treasure?"

"It was more of a... 'Here, hold onto this for me and wait on the park bench'... kind of situation," A. D. Hare, MD stammered, taking another cautious step back.

THE GNURETTE FIDDLED WITH THE TREASURE CHEST. "WE NEED A KEY! SNARF!"

ALL EYES TURNED TO A. D. HARE, MD. ONLY THE WHALEZHEIMER'S STARED AT THE CEILING.

"HERE IT IS. NO NEED TO PANIC,"
SAID A. D. HARE, MD CALMLY, PULLING A SMALL KEY FROM HIS POCKET.

THE GNURETTE SNATCHED THE KEY EAGERLY.
"CLICK, CLACK, LOCK, UNLOCK!" IT MUTTERED EXCITEDLY.

WITH TREMBLING HANDS, IT SLID THE KEY INTO THE LOCK, TURNED IT LEFT. THEN RIGHT.
THEN LEFT AGAIN. ONE MORE TURN TO THE RIGHT.

FINALLY, WITH AN EXAGGERATED FLOURISH, IT FLUNG THE CHEST OPEN.

BOOM!

A DEAFENING SOUND FILLED THE ROOM
AS AN INKY BLACK VOID ERUPTED FROM THE CHEST, COILING LIKE SMOKE.

THE DARKNESS WRITHED AND SURGED,
WRAPPING ITSELF AROUND THE GNURETTE IN A SUFFOCATING EMBRACE.

"SNAAAARF!" THE GNURETTE SHRIEKED AS THE VOID
YANKED IT INSIDE WITH A SHARP HISS.

THEN, DARKNESS.

SILENCE FELL. THICK, HEAVY, UNNATURAL SILENCE.

IN THE DISTANCE, A FAINT LIGHT FLICKERED.

"Who am I speaking to?" asked Dr. Fish softly,
his voice calm and measured as the room gradually brightened.

"Hoo? Click, Clack! Snarf!" came the familiar, jittery response.

"Ah, it's you," said Dr. Fish with a small smile.
"I missed you at our last therapy session. Where have you been?"

"On a treasure hunt, Hoo? Chasing a thief with some folks.
A few, well... let's just say they didn't quite make it. Snarf!
But... where are the others now?"

DR. FISH NODDED, HIS EXPRESSION UNCHANGED AS HE JOTTED A NOTE INTO HIS FILE.

HE REACHED BENEATH HIS DESK AND SLID A SLEEK,

FULL-LENGTH MIRROR INTO THE CENTER OF THE ROOM.

"THEY DON'T EXIST."

"HOLY HANDSCOOP. CLICK, CLACK!"

SHOUTED THE MULTIPERSOPANTHER AS HE SAW HIS REFLECTION.

AND THE MORAL OF THE STORY:
A LITTLE LAUGHTER CAN CURE A LOT OF WORRY.

THIS ALSO APPLIES TO LEAVING A REVIEW ONLINE.

OKAY, OKAY... THAT WAS A BIT OF A SHAMELESS ATTEMPT TO COLLECT SOME STARS - BUT IF IT WORKS, THANK YOU!

Dedicated to all those who face mental health challenges,
and to those who support them with unwavering care and love.

May your worries, if only for a brief moment, have been replaced by a smile.

Sometime in November 2024

Made in the USA
Las Vegas, NV
01 December 2024

bc37451b-a6a3-4145-a70c-04025e5d16fbR01